The $27 … een Re … on

Will Consumers Buy It?

John Redwood

The $275 Trillion Green Revolution – Will Consumers Buy It?

John Redwood

Cover by

Amelia Costley

Published by Bite-Sized Books Limited 2023
16 High Holborn, London, WC1V 6BX England
Registered in the UK. Company Registration
No: 9395379

ISBN: 978-1-7385584-2-1

Contents

Chapter 1

Background

We live in revolutionary times. World leaders and officials from the governments of the world meet in COP conferences to chart a course to net zero. Carbon is to be phased out rapidly. We are told we are following the science. Too much human generated CO_2 will warm the world too much. The climate changes that could result need to be prevented.

Joe Biden's America joins hands with the European Union in declaring war on carbon dioxide. A clever China agrees in principle and corners the market in many green products, whilst still increasing her output of the unpopular gas.

The protagonists strike an optimistic tone. They assure us the revolution will be carried through with a wide range of new green jobs. They hold out the promise of skilled people running windmill and battery factories, joyously powering the revolution of their dreams. They comment little on the other side, as they effectively sign the redundancy notices of all those in the oil and gas business, in drilling technology, in internal combustion engines, conventional ships, planes and vehicles, gas heating and much else. They have in mind a huge transition from the fossil fuel economy to the green electricity economy. They want us all to dump our diesel and petrol cars, replace our gas boilers, change our diet away from meat, give up foreign holidays and take to our bicycles.

All this will come with a huge price tag.

It is a costly business to replace our energy sources, the way we power industry, heat our homes and travel. There are forecasts of $275 trillion or more to complete the transition, three times current world annual GDP. There are plenty of arguments about who will pay. It is way beyond the power of governments alone, needing buy in from billions of consumers and millions of businesses using their own money.

The twentieth century shows us that mighty changes can happen quickly, and can raise living standards, creating more jobs than they destroy. Sometimes these changes are paid for by a private sector keen to switch to new technologies. Perhaps the fastest was the early century change from horse transport to motor transport. Out went the farriers and the horse minders, the water troughs and the hay baskets, and in came the petrol pumps, the garage mechanics and the world of road signs and traffic lights. The adoption was fast, thanks to the almost universal view that the car was so much more convenient than the horse. The big reduction in prices of cars achieved by Ford and others introducing mass production of basic models was a major spur. For those who could not afford even the entry level cars in the first half of the century there was the motor bus that brought the advantages of the new petrol and diesel engines to the many. As the century advanced more and more families could afford a car.

The conversion to carbon free has not developed the same momentum and pace yet that the petrol and diesel vehicle enjoyed. The problems include a perception that the newer green products are not as good as the fossil fuel products they wish to replace, and a view that the green items remain too expensive. Where the advent of the car, van and bus widened people's choices and offered longer range journeys to people who otherwise had to walk or find their way to a station, the arrival of the electric car or heat pumps does not offer the consumer any new service or capacity they do not already enjoy.

The problem with the green revolution is it comes from the top down. Government are the revolutionaries, not the hordes at the gates of power urging change. Government is trying to persuade or make people change their lifestyles without convincing them they will be better off if they do.

It is a paradox that a revolution should come from the very establishment that is threatened by it. Car companies making a good living selling excellent diesel and petrol cars queue up to decry their old products and promise a new range of electric cars as soon as they can get round to making them. Governments that enjoy huge revenues from oil and gas taxes, vehicle excise and fuel taxes sacrifice them with abandon, pretending that electric cars or electric heating will come tax free in contrast to their predecessors. The elite who have enjoyed dining out on the finest cuts of meat complain about the number of cattle on grassland. The powerful who have lived a charmed life flitting by first class jet to another five-star hotel in a remote country warn us off such a lifestyle. The press delights in uncovering hypocrisy, as some of the staunchest advocates of a new austerity or restraint in lifestyle fall foul of their own recommendations to others to cut their carbon miles.

It is time for a proper debate about this ersatz revolution, these grand plans often drawn up by people who think they should have some kind of exemption from the rules they set. So far, the green movement has spawned so many long-haul flights for delegates to arrive in air conditioned five-star hotels to urge the world to stop international flights and much else that many aspire to. It is now at the point where it has to translate aspirations into practical policies, and vague distant targets into shorter terms targets with bite.

The latest in the long series of UN sponsored climate change conferences, COP 28, was held in the United Arab Emirates, home to substantial oil and gas production. Enthusiastic green campaigners want to ban all new oil and gas drilling and agree plans to run down producing ones more quickly. The Conference battled over this issue. The background realities include the fact that 80% of the world's energy use is still fossil fuels. India and China, the two most populous countries, are both pursuing development plans based around using more fossil fuel this decade. Meanwhile the EU has economic policies centred around a green transition with regulatory and tax pressures to force the pace. The UK has gone furthest in reducing its CO2 output using carbon taxes and regulations. The US under President Trump greatly expanded its oil and gas extraction, whilst under President Biden there is a move to build more renewable energy. The Trump years did cushion the West from some of the impact of the Russian invasion of Ukraine, allowing the US to export more energy to Europe as well as producing most of its own needs. Germany has been fast to move from dependence on Russian gas by pipeline to importing more US gas as LNG. Doing so of course increases world CO 2 as conversion of gas to LNG and back again entails a lot of fossil fuel energy, as does the gas transport over long distances by tanker.

Chapter 2

The settled science

The scientific method is usually to produce a thesis or theory which best accords to known observations and data. This starting point then becomes a theory to test. Scientists seek to find more, better or different data. They probe the logic and the predictive power of the existing theory. Sometimes the initial theory is modified in minor ways, which over the years may accumulate considerable change. Sometimes a new theory is proposed which is widely agreed to have better logic and better fit with a wider range of data. Where a theory leads to predictive models, over time the models are refined or changed to get closer to providing high quality forecasts.

In the case of climate science, we are told the science is settled. They seem to mean by this that everyone agrees that there are greenhouse gases which over time if their volume and presence expands will cause the planet to heat up. I am not a scientist and have no reason to doubt this. I note that greenhouse gases include methane and water vapour as well as carbon dioxide.

Some of the critics additionally imply that the science is also settled so that increases in man-made carbon dioxide released to the atmosphere will cause global warming. This is linked to specific forecasts and to derived targets, to limit the warming to 1.5 degrees C or 2 degrees C by 2050. Of course, under the greenhouse gas theory this must be true if mankind adds to the stock of carbon dioxide and nothing else changes. It is even more true if other things change which also serve to raise the temperature.

Some of the critics of global warming theory argue that maybe other things are happening that might offset the impact of more man-made carbon dioxide. What if natural sources of carbon dioxide like volcanic activity are reducing as some offset to human carbon dioxide? What if there is a larger build-up of water vapour in the form of clouds, providing shadow and cover against the sun's rays more often and more effectively? What if the sun's intensity waned, with fewer flares? For any given country or region there could be changes in patterns of ocean currents that reduce rather than increase warming. There are issues over how you define a global average temperature. There are arguments over localised warming effects from human occupation concentrated in city regions distorting readings for temperatures. There are also climate scientists' answers to critical points.

It is not the purpose of this book to venture into this academic jungle. I am willing for the purpose of this book to accept that the "science is settled" and that man-made carbon dioxide is going to warm the planet up a bit. The aims are to look at the economic and social impact of this and above all to examine the impact of policies designed to limit or reduce carbon dioxide output.

It will ask if these policies actually reduce carbon dioxide in the way intended? It will ask if there are other unfortunate environmental effects from the pursuit of new technologies, products and materials. It will ask for whole life carbon accounting to deal with the danger that producing a new product and prematurely replacing on old one might mean more overall carbon dioxide is released when switching to an alleged greener version. It will also look at the benefits as well as the problems caused by the average temperature rising a bit, and the impact on food growing and vegetation from a more carbon dioxide rich atmosphere.

The aim is to provide a spur to more joined up thinking by the protagonists of a greener policy, to seek to ensure their actions are not contradictory in their own terms. The first necessity is for full life cycle carbon accounting. It is not a good idea to say that a particular vehicle or heating device lowers the carbon footprint of using it, if its manufacture imposes a substantial up front carbon cost and or if its end-of-life waste removal or recycling also imposes a high carbon cost. The new greener product has to stand comparison with the existing less green product over their whole lives from today, which must include the carbon impact of the manufacture of the new product and the scrapping of the old one. An electric vehicle, for example, will need a substantial user life on the original battery and a high enough yearly mileage to make it a greener product than simply running your existing internal combustion engine vehicle for longer. If you go over to heat pumps and find the temperature in winter too cool the calculation needs to include the environmental impact of top up heaters.

The second necessity is to get more accurate temperature data that the two sides in the debate can agree is fair and accurate. The concept of a single temperature figure for a world of such enormous climate diversity is a difficult one, so maybe there needs to be a series of agreed points that are accepted as official temperature sites where there is and will be little change over time in terms of population density and development to avoid contaminating the figures with other alterations.

Trying to test models from historical numbers is less easy to remedy, because historic temperature records are what they are. In future as governments seek to limit the rise to 1.5C, a very precise number, we need agreed methods of judging success.

The third is to conduct an accurate assessment of how successful the last fifty years of modelling and predicting have been. Critics of climate change theory have an impression that after the period of predicting a new ice age in the 1960s and 1970s predictions swung to forecasting more temperature increase than was experienced. It would be good to have some agreed data to resolve this issue.

The fourth is to see if there are unfortunate side effects from the climate change cure or fix that we need to eliminate or minimise. Some people are worried about the methods of mining and processing essential materials for batteries and other green products. Some are concerned that the job losses and business failures that could result from the removal of the fossil fuel economy will create new areas of deprivation, unemployment and poverty. Some think people will not be willing to make the large and permanent changes to lifestyle the new green imperatives require.

It does not make a lot of sense to close heavy fossil fuel using industry in one country like the UK to meet a national CO2 target, only to import the products from elsewhere entailing more fossil fuel energy use and more CO2 output. Switching to imports burdens the world with more CO2 generating transport to carry raw materials and finished goods over longer distances.

Chapter 3

The car is my freedom

As soon as people could afford cars, they bought them. The rich did not wish to cling to their horses and carriages, seeing the scope for faster and more comfortable travel from the newcomer. Those on lower incomes were impatient for cheaper, modest versions to give them the same convenience and range the rich enjoyed. The need for cheaper cars drove industrial change. Ford pioneered factory automation to alter a handmade coach-built product into a mass-produced precision piece of engineering at a much-reduced cost. The great car manufacturers competed to produce the best and cheaper vehicles. We went from Model T to Volkswagen Beetle, from Citroen 2CV to Austin Mini, from the Morris 8 to the Ford Anglia as cars for the many tripped off the production lines.

Young people saw the car as a ticket to freedom. Families saw the car as the means of getting away for days out and holidays, as well as the means to get to work or the shops. The second-hand car market helped give more people access at lower prices. With the advent of driver testing most young people wanted to pass their test as soon as they could after hitting the permitted age.

Today young people campaign vigorously on climate change issues, but many also stay wedded to the idea of personal transport. Being dependent on parents to offer a lift, or on public transport in many parts of the country where there is no tube and infrequent buses is not popular with many young people. The inconvenience gives them the urge to pass a driving test. Many would be happy with an electric vehicle but find them currently too dear. It will take time for the price to fall of the new ones and for a larger second-hand market to emerge with older and cheaper versions.

The battle of personal transport is one of the seminal contests the green revolutionaries think they need to win. To them it is obvious that people should walk and cycle more, use trains and buses and preferably not bother to buy a car. This is a particularly urban green view where people in densely populated city areas with great services and frequent public transport can indeed live without a car every day to get them to work, the shops and entertainment. For most people living in smaller towns, villages, hamlets and more distant suburbs there is no frequent public transport to meet their needs. Nor are there the services, restaurants, bars, cafes, shops, events and services within walking or cycling distance of their door. Most of us need a car to get to the shops, the train station, a local restaurant, a hairdresser or whatever.

The Green revolution in its government incarnation has seen that, for many people, ditching the car is not an option, so they are investing political capital and taxpayers' money in promoting the electric alternative to the internal combustion engine. In order for this to work in their own terms a number of important requirements need to be met.

The first is the electricity supply needs to be entirely based on renewables. An electric car is not a zero-carbon generator when working if its battery is recharged overnight from a power station burning fossil fuels. Most days the UK uses all the renewable power available, burning more gas to top up with fossil fuels as additional demand is called from the grid. Adding another electric car just adds to demand for more fossil fuelled electricity to recharge it. Burning the fossil fuel in a power station and then transmitting it with plenty of energy loss from generation and transmission is not a good idea compared to burning the fossil fuel directly in a conventional car engine.

The second is the lifetime impact of the carbon dioxide given off in producing the raw materials, components and assembly of the electric car needs to be placed into the calculation. Some figures show that if someone decides to continue running their diesel or petrol car for longer with a relatively low mileage it will be less carbon intensive than buying a newly minted electric car.

The third is any displacement of travel which may occur. If an electric car owner decides it is not suited for some journeys which they used to do by petrol car, then the green impact of the alternative needs to be taken into account. If, for example, a long journey is thought too difficult by electric car the person may substitute a taxi to and from stations and a train journey or may hire a car for the whole journey.

The consumer has other preoccupations. The first is price. Electric cars, like cars in general before them, have started more from the expensive end. The world's best known and so far best-selling western brand is Tesla. Their cars are aimed at the well off and rich, competing against luxury brands. There are now smaller and more realistically priced vehicles, but even so they tend to be at a premium price to conventional competitors.

Some countries have tried to jump start the market by offering substantial discounts or subsidies. Norway is the most advanced with considerable subsidies producing relatively high electric vehicle penetration. Other countries have not been able to afford such huge discounts and the loss of revenues which the advent of many electric cars bring. Consumers are also nervous, realising that introductory subsidies and discounts are all very well but at some point, government has to recoup its losses and find a way of taxing the electric vehicle as much as it currently taxes the petrol and diesel.

The second is range. Early electric cars had a range of under 100 miles compared to the 400-500 mile range of the typical family diesel. More recent battery improvements have produced enhanced ranges, without yet being able to match a traditional car easily. There are also disputes about how the range is calculated and how reliable the forecast might be. If a driver goes out at night needing lights, wants the radio on, has to put on the wipers because it is raining and needs the heater there are large additional calls on the power in the battery. If the driver gets stuck in a traffic jam that too can cut the range. Manufacturers' claims on range are likely to become matters of dispute and possible litigation.

The third is the time it takes to recharge. With a petrol or diesel car refuelling takes five minutes to fill the tank and pay the bill. A full recharge of a battery vehicle may take many hours. Accelerated fast charging may give someone enough charge in say twenty to thirty minutes. There are still arguments about how responsive and easy to recharge batteries are over their lives. It is true this is no hassle if you can recharge at home overnight and if your normal journeys each day are well within the car's range. There remains the issue of how you handle longer journeys or recharging when away from home.

The fourth is the availability of recharging points. Of course, this issue can be resolved over time by the introduction of many more charging points, but in the build-up phase this is a real issue affecting tendencies to buy electric. In the UK today there are limited numbers of charging points.

People planning longer journeys in electric cars can plan in advance where they need to reach to find a convenient recharge location. All too often when they arrive, they find they are not compatible with their vehicle, or they are temporarily out of order, or they are very busy. Being busy is not like a petrol pump where the person in front will clear in a short space of time, as the car in front may need a serious charge. The prices of fast charge are also often several times the cost of domestic electricity, eroding one of the perceived advantages of the electric vehicle.

The fifth is battery life. The battery is a major part of the cost of the vehicle. Some argue that if you use accelerated chargers often that cuts the life of the battery. The industry is only gradually building up data on how long you can expect your car battery to give good service. Batteries do deteriorate over time, limiting performance and range as they lose some of their original power.

The customer who remains interested in the electric vehicle after considering these issues will have some positives in mind.

The first is running cost. If you can rely on topping up the battery by recharging at home at domestic power rates it may well be cheaper to fuel an electric car. If you need to use public chargers there is higher VAT and higher power prices to contend with. For society as a whole the cost of conventional electricity compared to petrol or diesel is higher because it is a secondary fuel with more energy loss. The electric car does need 100% renewable electricity for it to be worthwhile.

The second is if the owner has a garage or standing area close to the house with a suitable electric car power socket then it is easier to recharge the car than take a petrol or diesel to a filling station. This assumes never going beyond the range of the vehicle for the combined outbound and home route.

The third is the owner can feel they are making their contribution to net zero by substituting an electric car for a fossil fuel machine, though for this to be true the other issues mentioned above need to be resolved in a green direction.

So far when examining this balance of issues most people conclude they are not ready to make a commitment to an electric vehicle. All those living without garages and driveways are especially disadvantaged from using an electric car. Norway suggests that if government made a big financial contribution that could make a difference. Launching products that genuinely had much better ranges on a single charge would make a difference. More honest information about battery life and recharging options could make a difference if it was good news.

Electric vehicles are currently around 1% of the total vehicle stock of the world, with fast growth in new sales on a low base. Governments think electric vehicles are the answer and have decided to use a combination of subsidies, regulation and advocacy to promote them. Several countries are considering banning the sale of new diesel and petrol cars as early as 2030. This is drawing them into considering just how much they are prepared to spend to try to bring this about. The fledgeling electric industry is pressing for state involvement in subsidising their prices, help with putting in a charging infrastructure and beefing up electricity supply to meet the possible large increment to demand.

So far, the electric car is most likely to be favoured by a rich person living in a city where they can afford the vehicle, do not need long range and have ways of recharging it overnight. It is least likely to be considered by someone on low income in a house without a drive or garage, and especially in a rural area where they need longer range to get through the typical day.

The UK, Germany and EU have recently delayed phase out of new petrol and diesel vehicles until 2035. The UK is still introducing extra taxes on car makers if they sell too many petrol and diesel cars relative to their electric ones. This places the manufacturers in a difficult position as many consumers are still unwilling to buy electric.

Some Tesla consumers buy a Tesla but also have a petrol or diesel car for longer journeys which is a luxury most cannot afford. All the time fossil fuel is needed in power stations to recharge batteries it is difficult to see the advantage of these policies. The extra CO2 from their manufacture and likelihood many will be imported from China adds to the dangers of the policy of trying to force the pace of switching.

Chapter 4

Powering down the climate

The early attention of governments in their long pursuit of net zero was turned to the electricity generating industry itself. Large utility businesses with stable and good cashflows could be regulated to change the way they generated power. Governments lighted onto the dominance of coal, gas and oil as fuels in power stations and required gradual shifts from these sources to renewables. Coal was identified as the most carbon intensive, as well as needing substantial cleansing of waste gases emerging from the furnaces. European countries determined to force the closure of all coal stations, with the UK for example almost complying in the last decade. During a recent windless period, the UK did need to use three old coal stations again to cover some of the renewable shortfall. Gas power stations have not been put under the same pressure as they achieve higher efficiencies and therefore generate less carbon per unit of output.

The preferred options to fossil fuel were solar and wind. When the transformation began these ways of producing electricity were considerably dearer than fossil fuel, so a variety of subsidies were offered and preferential treatment on the grid in calling up these sources of power when they were available. Today the green industries claim solar and onshore wind are close to parity in cost or even cheaper, as the manufacturing costs of solar panels and windmills has come down through improved designs and the economies of scale. As larger wind turbine blades have been produced the mechanical efficiency of the turbines has been raised, increasing the amount of power produced for the same investment substantially.

The claim to cheaper is queried by sceptics. They point to the need for substantial back up power in case the wind drops or the sun retreats and seek to include the construction and maintenance costs of this capacity as part of the cost of renewables. There are also disagreements about the true cost of combined cycle gas. It is cheaper if it is run as baseload generating power all the time. If you keep switching it on and off the power becomes dearer, as the producer seeks to blend gas power in with erratic renewable power where the renewable power takes priority when it is available. The priority use of renewable power gives it a pricing advantage.

Electorates in democracies often prefer offshore to onshore wind. Wind farms are said to be noisy to live near, to damage the view of otherwise beautiful countryside, and to be tough on birds. It is not always easy for an investor to get planning agreement from a local community to placing a sizeable wind farm in a locality. Offshore wind farms far enough offshore or off a remote enough shore to avoid offending are more popular. They are also quite a lot dearer to introduce, needing longer and stronger legs to be stable in the raging seas.

Solar arrays are becoming a more common sight. They offer a farm owner or tenant an additional income for part of their land that can exceed the farm income value. Solar panels can also be incorporated into domestic and commercial buildings to provide some of the power they need and to supply to the grid when they produce an excess.

China produces 30% of the world's total carbon dioxide emissions. It is true China has been an early adopter of solar and wind power. It is also true that to keep the lights on and the fast-growing industrial economy powered up China has in recent years continued to dig more coal and build more coal powered stations. There is likely to be a growing interest in when China will reach peak coal and start to do what the advanced world has been doing for some time, running down the amount of power derived from coal. So far China has made an imprecise promise to end the construction of coal power stations outside China, but not at home.

The world as a whole has a long way to go to derive most of its power from renewable sources. Currently solar and wind are only around 5% of total world electricity output. The more advanced countries in putting in renewables are China, the USA, Germany, Spain, India and the UK. The leaders are talking about trying to get to 40% this decade. Meanwhile the growing demands for power to accommodate world growth, to provide for a massive expansion of electric vehicles, and to allow more homes and businesses to be heated by electricity means doubling or trebling the totals that are needed to keep up.

The scale of the planned electric revolution means big decisions have to be taken and large investment commitments made to get the power to every home and business premise on the scale needed. Grids and local networks will need more cable capacity to take doubled or trebled electricity demands. Many homes will need a fast charger socket for the car. Many streets will need car charger sockets where people need to leave their cars overnight parked in the road. There will be some further development of battery technology, with some thinking the car battery will become part of the domestic system. Not only will the car battery be mainly recharged from the home system after use, but the car battery could provide stand by power at peak periods for the home where the general system was stretched.

System and grid management is made much more difficult by the presence of so much more interruptible or unreliable power. Both wind and solar are very variable and difficult to predict. Electricity systems will need standbys and supplements to smooth the output. This can come from hydro schemes using stored water, from battery stores or from conventional power stations if they can be brought on stream quickly when needed. In the UK the Dinorwig pump storage scheme is quick acting. The UK also now relies on an ability to import power through interconnectors from France, Belgium and Norway. These too could prove unreliable for a variety of reasons.

The French have already threatened Jersey with cutting off their power which is supplied by submarine cable as part of a fishing dispute. The reliability of grid power within the EU is dependent on the continuing goodwill of foreign energy suppliers which provide them with substantial gas. The French have a big task to decide how to replace their ageing fleet of nuclear reactors, whilst Germany still has coal as well as gas on the system which needs to be taken out to meet their climate change objectives. The EU as it embarks on its electrical revolution will need greatly increased power at exactly the same time as the UK will. In September 2023 the main French interconnector was interrupted by a major fire at the Sellindge electricity facility for the link. There may be more times when an absence of wind or solar power in the UK is also being experienced elsewhere in Europe.

Most governments have found tackling the electricity industry the easiest part of walking the road to net zero. Electricity is in the main produced by a few very large companies in each jurisdiction using a centralised model. Distribution takes place through a unified national grid. The companies are used to strict regulation and government awareness of their customer relations, returns on capital, planning and siting of generating and distribution assets and controls on emissions. It was a relatively straightforward move from regulating flue gases and priority call up to supply the grid to forcing through an overriding priority to reduce carbon dioxide output whilst producing power.

Some have used carbon prices to provide cost penalties to producing electricity from fossil fuels. Some have heavily subsidised renewable competitors to get them started within the system. Systems have been adjusted through formulae, carbon taxes and renewable subsidies to call up and use as much renewable power as possible.

Despite curbing fossil fuel in generation being relatively low hanging fruit, heavy industrial users like China and Germany have still been unwilling to go as far as the world community would like in decarbonising power. China is still building new coal stations and is adding to the fleet as it wants a reliable form of power alongside the volatile and erratic wind and solar sources. Germany is declining to phase out her coal stations before 2038. Neither great industrial power buys fully into the new world of renewable, batteries and grid management as substitutes for reliable baseload power from predictable fossil fuels. The June 2021 G7 Communique on power stated, "Coal power generation is the single biggest cause of global temperature increases." It went on to urge, "system integration of variable renewable energy, energy storage, flexible power plants, hydrogen, as well as demand side management, smart grids, and related infrastructure including the accommodation of sustainable biofuels and hydrogen."

Much of this is still an aspiration.

Customers are not willingly taking to demand management if that means penal prices at certain times of day or even restrictions on use. Grid managers struggle with too much interruptible power suddenly being unavailable, whilst we await sufficient roll out of larger batteries to make a useful contribution to supply. On a cold day with little wind or sun the advanced countries are still very reliant on fossil fuels. Many UK customers refuse to have a smart meter though they are supplied free of charge to the individual user, paid for out of a levy on all bills. Consumers are suspicious of how they might be used to regulate demand.

Chapter 5

Hydrogen - the new green kid on the block

The work on trying to electrify the car is difficult enough. Trying to electrify the heavy truck or the passenger airplane is even more difficult. Large trucks are usually fuelled by diesel engines which provide large amounts of torque to pull heavy loads. Experiments with batteries have shown that to get a battery large enough and powerful enough imposes a further large weight on the truck which makes it difficult to get load pulling and acceleration up to acceptable levels. This has led to the search for more environmentally acceptable fuels for something more like a traditional internal combustion engine, or for ways of creating electricity within the moving vehicle.

The current great hope is hydrogen gas. People have built and put into service buses that run on hydrogen-based propulsion systems. Glasgow operates such buses. Barcelona and some German cities are also on this route. Hydrogen is clean when burnt, producing water as the waste. It is not that easy to handle and needs storage under pressure to get enough of it into a realistic space. Hydrogen is more than three times less dense in energy than natural gas by volume and 2700 times less than gasoline, so large quantities are needed to power a vehicle. Its energy density is good if it is stored at high pressure. If it is held in liquid form, it is much compressed, but needs careful handling and a temperature below minus 253 degrees. There also needs to be facilities to shift it back to compressed gas form for use. It is a secondary fuel, needing to be made from water and electricity.

Some trucks run using hydrogen as a fuel for an internal combustion style engine. More of the buses and lighter vehicles use fuel cell technology, where hydrogen is the fuel used to generate continuous power rather than rely on a large battery. All these systems are thought to provide a better power to weight performance than a large in vehicle battery for propulsion.

In order to qualify as fully green, the hydrogen has to be produced by electrolysis from water using renewable power. As a secondary fuel with less energy intensity than the fuel it replaces it will be dearer and less efficient than the underlying natural gas. Natural gas has become the preferred fuel for much space heating and many industrial processes, especially in the UK and Europe where the winters are long and cold requiring a lot of energy for heating. Many owners of gas boilers for their homes are keeping them, hoping that if the green transition is going to bite on them, they will be able to convert their existing natural gas boilers to hydrogen gas and receive a piped supply of that instead of the present fossil fuel delivery. Some modern natural gas boilers would be easy to convert in such circumstances.

The task of such a change would be large. As the Ministers for Climate Change and the Environment confided in their Communique prior to June 2021 Leaders' Summit in Cornwall "We recognise the importance of renewable and low carbon hydrogen on the pathway to net zero. We will step up efforts to advance commercial scale hydrogen from low carbon and renewable sources across our economy including support for fuel cell deployment globally." Since then, the EU has required the roll out of hydrogen fuelling points along all its highways in anticipation of demand for trucks and buses.

Producing large amounts of hydrogen will require much more renewable power. Turning it into hydrogen does allow the storage of renewable power in a more useful form, allowing capture of wind or solar energy when demand for the electricity itself is low. It will need adaptation of the current gas pipe system and substantial installations in depots and garages for commercial vehicles and buses to make more of a reality of the hydrogen revolution.

The EU, US and UK are also working on synthetic fuels and sustainable aviation fuels. No-one is planning large passenger jets to fly long distances on a battery. Targets are being set to gradually increase the proportion of sustainable or synthetic fuel in aviation spirit, allowing continuing use of existing jet engines. Trial quantities of a fuel which is carbon neutral have been created which can power older cars without modification of the engines. So far, the leading countries in these areas continue to encourage and develop both electric vehicles and low or no carbon fuels for conventional engines.

Chapter 6

Vegetarians only please

The UK's Climate Change Committee wants to reshape the landscape in the image of net zero. Around one quarter of net emissions of greenhouse gases come from farming. The bulk of those come from animal husbandry as the world indulges its taste for beef, lamb, pork and dairy products. The production system uses substantial energy on fertiliser production, feedstuff production and meat preparation. In addition, the animals themselves generate a lot of methane during their lives. Methane is said to do 100 times the damage the same quantity of carbon dioxide would do, so it is a super greenhouse gas.

The worldwide industry faces the same challenge as in the UK. Large meat and dairy companies are under pressure to show how they plan to get to net zero. Most cannot offer a clear route. Some make strong promises to manage what they can manage. They are looking to source their power and fertilisers from renewable sources to cut the output of bad gases. They promise to cut their waste and to help their customers cut theirs. It is difficult to see how they can eliminate the methane from their animals and have to offer instead a move to more offsets for the greenhouse gas they will still release. They do try out methane reducing diets for cattle.

The UK Committee acknowledges it can only reduce and not eliminate all of this. It proposes as a first objective getting consumers to reduce their intake of meat and dairy products by one fifth. The problem with this is as people become better off their consumption of expensive foods from the meat and dairy industries rises. If the UK manages to restrain too much extra spending on meat and dairy as wages go up, we will still face the likelihood of this happening on a huge scale as people in emerging economies reach better levels of income.

They suggest that by the joint efforts of producers, retailers and consumers food waste could also be cut. Too much meat ends up in the rubbish at the end of the week. Restaurants and cafes also have difficulties in eliminating waste as people may have varying tastes and appetites around their menus.

Work is well advanced on finding more substitutes and similar tasting products for meat by using plant inputs like soya. Some are also trying insect farming to provide less methane producing protein.

The landscape would be recast with much more emphasis on tree growing. The UK Committee wants 90-120 million extra trees planted each year as 10% of farmland is turned over to forestry. It also wants to see more peatland established, with the restoration of peat bogs which are seen as carbon sinks. The UK government has adopted much of this agenda and is pushing ahead with grant and support schemes for farmers to rewild parts of their estates, to recreate peat bogs and to plant many trees. There is less discussion or enthusiasm for growing the plant alternatives to dairy and meat needed to feed a growing population.

Worldwide there is more interest in soya production, one of the most common meat substitutes, alongside various fruits, mushrooms, quorn and tofu and plant milks. The challenge is to persuade the new rich of the emerging world to go back to diet necessities of the time when they were on low incomes and could not afford the meat and dairy alternatives.

The Green movement is coming to see the large meat and dairy interests as an even bigger obstacle to their task than the oil, coal and gas companies that have now accepted the need to go on a journey to net zero. The food companies are not yet producing and promoting an alternative to meat in the way the energy companies are now promoting electricity from renewable sources. Consumers who have been told so often of the need to cut their car journeys have not yet had the same intense pressure exerted on their diets.

The climate change Greens link up with the animal welfare campaigners. There are strong moves now to improve or close down factory farms that provide poor conditions for the captive animal. The better off can afford to buy the free range or grass-fed product, but bigger moves in that direction will leave those on lower incomes shut out from so much meat and will cut overall output. Many of the arguments over international trade are fostered by those who want more lower income people to be able to afford meat produced by the most efficient producers of the world, whilst animal welfare considerations argue against long distance transit and factory methods of production.

It is difficult to know how far governments will wish to press the case for less meat and more vegetables. They can of course force changes of diet for all but the rich by taxes and price mechanisms. There is already a well-established practice of agricultural protectionism in the advanced countries, who seek to keep out cheaper agricultural products from countries with more mechanised farms, better soils and climate. The system of tariffs and subsidies could be rejigged to be tough on meat and kinder on the preferred green alternatives. There will be issues about over-use of the soils for key crops like soyabeans. The absence of many farm animals makes it difficult to access natural fertiliser and reduces the scope for rotation between grazing land and arable, and between grass growing for fodder and growing arable crops.

The case that says providing protein through the medium of farm animal meat is inefficient as a way of using the riches of the earth may be true, but it does provide variety, protect soils from monoculture and reflects the teeth and stomachs of people that are adapted to eating a mixture of meat and vegetable.

More to the point there is the issue of dietary choices, where many people regard a meat or fish diet as being preferable. Indeed, those on low incomes aspire to being able to afford more such protein as their circumstances improve. There are also large economic interests invested fully in the protein business, from meat producers through butchers to great chefs and great restaurants.

It is also true that an increasing number of people are opting for vegetarian diets. There are many more good dishes and choices of vegetarian food available. Nonetheless the large majority are wedded to their beefburgers and their steaks and will need a lot of persuading that they need to change. This may prove to be another bridge too far for green governments to cross, if they decide to go head-to-head with the powerful interests of the meat industry and the hospitality industry's use of their products.

The increase in carbon dioxide does help crop yields as CO 2 is important in plant development. Global warming will change the pattern of agriculture worldwide. Colder less favourable climates for plants and animal husbandry will become more benign. It will be possible to grow grapes further north shifting wine production for example. Whilst some places may become too hot and dry for farming without extensive irrigation and shade barriers, other places will become more productive. The latest agricultural revolution is anyway enabling fruit, vegetable and flower growers to produce in controlled greenhouse conditions on a large scale, eliminating the impact of weather on their crops.

What does a green holiday look like?

The holiday is perhaps the central clash between green governments and their voters. Many people think a good holiday involves taking the family car to an airport, jetting off to somewhere in the sun and staying in a good hotel near the sea or beauty spots which you wish to visit. The travel is very carbon intensive. The lifestyle on arrival can also be so. There is the hotel air conditioning to make the heat tolerable. There is the fancy food, and the carbon dioxide generated by sustaining the hotel and all its staff. To governments this should be the most easily avoidable generation of carbon dioxide. To the voters this is the indulgence that makes the work tolerable or worthwhile, the pay-off for all the rest they do to help the economy and pay the family bills.

Government attacks on jet travel for pleasure is made more difficult for them by their own passion to meet likeminded people in similar positions in other countries. Government is one of the biggest users of jet travel and good hotels, as Ministers and senior officials, advisers and contractors jet around the world talking to each other in person. It leads to many annoyed photo exchanges and quips on social media around the theme of don't do as I do, do as I say. Government after all has an easier substitute than the holiday maker. They can talk to their counterparties on a zoom call. The iPad does not let you get a swim or enjoy the sunshine in a faraway land as a holidaymaker.

An approved green holiday would require the deletion of jet travel, as that is such a carbon intensive thing to do. It would argue for holidays much nearer to home. Instead of millions of UK people flying abroad for the sun, they would seek relaxation at UK resorts and take a chance on the weather. Instead of large numbers of foreign travellers coming to London for the culture and the sights, they would stay closer to their homes. Some of the tourist industry would be saved by more local people using it instead of long-range travellers. Some of it which specialises in particular foreign travellers would wither. The large hotels would need to adapt to a greener way of offering service, Meals would need less animal protein. Heating and cooling systems would have to be driven by green energy. There would be fewer organised trips over longer distances from the hotel, and more concentration on walking and activities that do not require much mechanical power to be expended.

These are not changes people are wanting to make on a large scale. It will require a lot of government patience to persuade enough to make an impact. It is more likely impatient governments will seek to regulate leisure flying more, making it difficult for companies to offer low and discounted fares. Aviation can be priced higher by landing charges, fuel duties, carbon offset requirements and the rest. Gradually the exotic overseas holiday will be priced for the rich, not for the average. The package holiday, the cheap air fares, the two weeks in the sun will need to rethought by an industry under direction to slash its carbon output.

Chapter 7

Heating and cooling

Space heating is the new frontier that governments are approaching. A family's largest contribution to the carbon dioxide increases of the planet may be from their central heating system. Some are still using solid fuel. Coal is the biggest rogue in the pack of fossil fuels used worldwide. Homes with coal fires or coke boilers will be under pressure to change. Most people in the UK rely on gas boilers for the heat. These too are thought to be unacceptable going forward. New homes are told to find substitutes, with an early phase out of gas boilers planned.

The big task is to persuade people with perfectly good serviceable gas boilers that they should accelerate the change. There is a dispute over what the change should entail. Some favour heat pumps, others wish to wait until there is a green gas available to burn. In the UK an early move by the government to phase out all new gas boilers by 2030 and to require heat pumps has now been postponed. A heat pump installation costs well into five figures which is not realistic for most households, and is a big turn off from any idea you might substitute your gas boiler before it is close to the end of life. It is also unclear just how green it would be to require the mass scrapping of existing gas boilers alongside the production of new heat pumps in sufficient quantities.

All such change brings with it its own heavy resource cost to produce the new systems and burdens the carbon accountants with a substantial carbon dioxide debit which needs to be included in the life cost calculation for the new heating system. Nor does a heat pump easily satisfy the need for decent standards of warmth in winter homes in the UK. The householder may well need to top up the heat with some form of electric heating. This too comes with a carbon cost all the time part of the grid supply of energy is based on power generated from fossil fuels.

Some people think the answer is to await the development of hydrogen as a fuel. It should be possible to route hydrogen through the existing gas pipelines. Gas boilers could be converted at relatively low cost to take the new fuel. Some modern ones are already capable of running on hydrogen. The hydrogen of course would need to be green hydrogen, generated itself from water using wind or solar renewable energy. This system would need a further expansion of electrical power, as would heat pumps needing electricity to top up heating. Commercial organisations are looking harder at introducing their own solar panels or wind generated power at their premises or at reassuring green aware customers and financiers that they are taking trouble to buy green electricity for their heating and cooling needs.

There are renewed arguments over wood burning stoves. Many people like the extra warmth and the look of a fire in the grate as a focus for a winter room. They can also be useful back up in case of failure of central heating systems. Some greens argue burning wood is a generator of CO2 and should be disallowed. Others say that if the wood is from a sustainable source where replacement wood will be planted for that cut down it meets the net zero requirement. The CO 2 from burning it will be offset by the CO 2 absorbed by growing replacements. In the UK the

Drax power station is approved for net zero as a wood burning facility. The wood or biomass used in the plant is imported so it does not count against the UK CO 2 given the national carbon accounting conventions.

Changing the way we heat and cool our properties is the single most important step that could be taken to reduce CO2 output, after the conversion of all electricity generation.

In contrast the digital revolution is bottom up, not top down.

The digital revolution has swept on as the green revolution stays largely in the minds of governments and legislators. It has not taken a new cat's cradle of taxes and subsidies to get people to acquire a mobile phone. It has not taken new rules and laws to persuade people to buy a laptop or an iPad. People have freely chosen to spend their own money on downloading movies from digital service providers, to spend money on internet links so they can keep in touch using social media and can download a range of apps to assist them in their daily lives on their phone.

The digital giants grew their businesses by shrewd marketing, by defining new needs for people, and by a liberal dose of "free" service paid for by adverts or by business users only. The internet providers have rapidly taken market share off conventional shops with their powerful online retailing offers. The advertising market has shifted from traditional media dominance to social media online. Entertainment is readily available as a download and businesses are keen to use internet conferencing facilities for meetings.

It is true that the pandemic boosted the market share of many of these providers of remote services. As people were forced to work from home and to enjoy more domestic entertainment, so the internet providers picked up many new customers. As people were restricted in going to the shops, they could readily turn to the online offer. However, this merely accelerated trends that were already apparent before the pandemic and the lockdowns struck. Many people had already opted for more of an online life. The lockdowns forced people who had been tec shy to buy iPads and smartphones and to try their hands at online shopping and entertainment.

This experience contrasts so starkly with the green products. There was no similar rush to buy electric vehicles, heat pumps and meat substitutes, even though governments all claimed that the pandemic meant we could now build back better. They usually defined this as creating a green economy and continuing the task of demolishing the older industries and processes that were fossil fuel dependent.

So, what is the big difference between the popular bottom up spread of the digital revolution and the slow and sticky spread of the top-down green revolution? It comes down to affordability and utility. Many have saved up or bought a contract for mobile phones because they offer them access to a world of social contact and information they want. It is an enhancement of someone's life that they can see a moving map or get weather or entertainment information on the move with a mobile phone. It is an improvement in a busy life if you can look something up quickly online and order it direct, with a likely delivery the next day. Many people want the choice of a movie to download and view rather than having to accept the choices of established media.

In contrast the green revolution offers things that are dearer or less desirable than things people already own. Most people in the UK heat their water and their homes from a gas boiler. All the time it works well they have no wish to rip it out and replace it with something different. They might be persuaded if the replacement meant a decent saving on the fuel bill but to achieve that they would want a product which was not too expensive and which was relatively easy to put into their home. The proposed heat pumps are very expensive, and not that effective at low temperatures. They might require expensive topping up with electric heating during cold spells, and anyway run off dearer electricity compared to cheaper gas. The supply industry is not well developed and many gas fitters who currently supply and maintain our boilers are sceptical about the new technology. All this militates against a take-off in demand for these products.

As we have seen people remain concerned about various issues over electric cars, which also remain expensive. It is quite a big move for someone to become a vegetarian, and many would see that as diminution in the variety and choice of food they eat. There are limits to how far governments in free societies can go in dictating to people how they should lead their lives.

Chapter 8

What would make us green revolutionaries?

Some people are more inclined to revolution, and some are more inclined to seek comfort and safety in conserving what they have. Those who like revolution might be attracted to the green version because it is so wide ranging and common amongst established governments and international bodies. Many other people see it as a threat. They do not want to change their diet, renew their car and rip out their heating. Some do not have the money to do so. Some do not want the disruption, some fear they will not understand or be able to cope with the different technologies on offer.

Some in the global establishment think the way to win more people over to the changes they want us to make is to launch a new Project Fear. If more people seriously thought their own home could be burned down by excessive heat in the atmosphere and a strong sun or if more thought their home might be washed away by unusual floods or sea level rise, then maybe more people would be prepared to take urgent and expensive action to save themselves. If each time there is a serious fire caused by sunlight or each time there are floods the media would help by claiming this is the result of global warming, then maybe more people would come to this conclusion.

In recent years there has been much reporting of extreme weather events as a sign that climate change is now going to accelerate and worsen our experiences of floods, forest fires and hotter weather. There is a reluctance to compare current bad examples of floods and fires with past extremities, and little interest in reporting the weather events like cold and damp summers that do not fit with the overall picture. The issue is made complex by the difficulty in deciding on a single set of numbers that capture world climate. California may be living through a heatwave whilst northern Europe is having relatively cool weather for the time of year. Past examples of the establishment using Project Fear tactics have not been very successful for those trying to make a case from their worries.

Let us assume that the scientific and political establishment does persuade enough people that climate change is all going in one direction towards a warmer world and persuades them that this will lead to unacceptable heatwaves and fires, to rising sea levels and floods.

There are still two further tasks for the governments to achieve.

The first is to get each individual to believe that what they do can make a difference. It is too easy for people to say that all the time China pours out more and more carbon dioxide any attempts to restrain will be futile. It is easy for people to feel helpless beneath the weight of evidence of a rising tide of carbon dioxide from the developing world as they understandably burn more fuel to catch up with our living standards, and a continued large output by advanced countries struggling to adjust without stopping people driving and cooking and heating their homes.

The second is to persuade people that there are changes they can make that will help, that are affordable and will still allow them to lead decent lives. The current range of products on offer is still not persuasive enough. People are scarred by the experience with diesel cars. Many adopted them in part because governments said they would be good for the environment, increasing fuel economy and so cutting carbon dioxide emissions. Subsequently government changed its mind.

There are worries lest throwing out an older car or heating system turns out to be less good for the planet thanks to the burden making the new one imposes, however much better it may be when running.

The discovery that electric cars still produce tyre and brake dust, so they do not remove particulate pollution, reveals the depth of concerns. Those who have advocated a greener approach have implied the switch to an electric car is to reduce particulates, which have all but been eliminated from the back of new petrol and diesel vehicles anyway thanks to improved combustion and exhaust treatment. It shows how the debate about carbon dioxide has been diverted to other important environmental matters, but not always in an accurate and helpful way.

Chapter 9

The move from long term pledges to specific actions

Governments have done the easy parts. Through a succession of international conferences most countries have signed the Treaty and agreed to progress to net zero. Many have agreed to get there by 2050. Now the journey gets harder. It is no longer thought good enough to promise net zero for a distant date without showing progress getting there and without spelling out in a detailed plan how the new tougher intermediate targets will be hit. Cops 26, 27 and 28 were all about the participating nations improving their national plans and showing what positive actions they will take to get to net zero faster. The conferences considered the future of coal, with many advocating eliminating coal from power generation and household grates whilst accepting a continuing if transitional role for specialist areas like steel production. They reviewed how far and fast they can go with switching away from meat and dairy products. Is natural gas best phased out or gradually converted to a mixture with more hydrogen? Can transport be electrified or does it too need some hydrogen substitutes for oil-based fuel?

There have been two particularly tough sets of arguments between the richer and the developing nations.

Will the richer countries accept the developing world needs to expand its use of fossil fuels before it is rich enough to go on transition to non-carbon-base activity? Or will the richer countries help the poorer countries accelerate transition by large grants and other financial support? Is the balance of challenge and achievement between the richer countries themselves fair, or are some getting trading advantage out of a slow and less expensive transition?

Whilst much of the debate is about leaving it to individual countries to develop and police their own plans, there are also some international issues to consider.

Should the world move to carbon border taxes? Governments are always looking for new sources of revenue, and this one has moral appeal. Shouldn't there be an extra levy on imports from countries that persist in emitting a large amount of carbon dioxide in the production of their cheaper exports? The EU and the US are considering such an impost. China will see that as a hostile act. Such a tax might succeed in diverting some purchases from international trade to domestic production, saving carbon dioxide on the transit, and allowing less carbon intensive production methods.

Can the world create any further incentives or penalties to get countries into line who are slow or reluctant to travel this road? It is most likely to result in further global aid and subsidy.

At COP 28 the nations did agree a new fund to pay compensation to poorer countries for the CO 2 emitted by the advanced nations. Whilst the principle was established the sums contributed so far have been small. The conference also urged richer countries to meet the promised $100bn a year of transfers to emerging economies to help with decarbonisation. This pledge has been around at successive COP s but so far, the annual sums have fallen short of the promise.

COP 28 claimed a breakthrough by saying that the world should transition away from fossil fuels. This was said to be an important advance, yet that was implied in all the work of previous conferences from the signing of the original Paris Treaty against climate change. The nations were unable to agree a text saying fossil fuels would be phased out. Many of the participants expressly or privately expect some fossil fuels to be a necessary part of the energy landscape in 2050. Net zero does not necessarily mean no fossil fuel use. Much work has gone into carbon offsets including carbon capture and storage.

Chapter 10

The energy shortages following the Russian invasion of Ukraine and other events

In the run up to COP26 the world was reminded how dependent on fossil fuels it still is. In September there was the perfect storm in energy markets. The USA lost gas and oil output thanks to the devastation created by Hurricane Ida. Russian gas exports were down, probably as President Putin decided to shock Germany and the EU in to signing large contracts for future supply through the newly completed NordStream 2 pipeline. Western Europe generated much less wind power as the weather entered a period of calm, forcing generators to use more gas. The revival of the Asian economies after lockdowns led to stronger demand for LNG gas to the east.

As a result, markets were very short of gas and the price more than trebled. Some industries shut down or reduced activity, struggling with sky high gas prices eclipsing modest margins.

The electricity markets too saw shortages and high prices. The two markets are interlinked, with gas a primary fuel that is much used in power generation. The reliance on wind was a weakness as the wind disappeared for a bit. There was a dash to re-open old coal power stations and stock up with more coal for those facilities in use.

Worse followed with the Russian invasion of Ukraine in February 2022. The West decided to impose sanctions and to seek to eliminate most Russian gas and oil from its own imports. This caused big surges in oil, gas and electricity prices and led the EU to require reductions in winter usage of power to reduce some of the stresses in the markets. Strides were taken to reorient Germany and others from piped Russian gas to imported LNG from the USA and elsewhere. There was no chance to complete an early switch to renewable electricity as so many EU homes and factories depend on gas. They had become reliant on relatively cheap piped Russian gas.

Today the oil and gas markets have settled down again. More Russian energy is sold to China and other non-western countries, whilst the US,

Norway, Qatar and others supply more to the European importers.

It was a sign that even the relatively easy transition from fossil fuels to renewables in electricity generation is still far from complete and fraught with problems. China has not started to curtail her use of coal. India and the USA still rely heavily on fossil fuels for electricity. The electrical revolution will need a very large expansion in electrical capacity to handle all the new cars, heating systems and industrial processes that will need renewable power. There also needs to be a better answer for back up when the wind does not blow and when the sun's contribution to solar is weak.

Chapter 11

The enormous scope of the ambition

The Green revolutionaries are nothing if not bold. They wish to change the way practically every factory is powered. They want to transform processes for making things like steel, ceramics, paper and glass. They want to change the way we travel, substituting entirely different cars and trucks for the petrol and diesel ones that are common. They want to end jet flying as we know it. They want to change the way we heat our homes, alter our diets, transform farms and the countryside, and much else.

All of this will prove very expensive. It will take trillions of dollars to switch so much energy from fossil fuel to renewable electricity. It will require huge increases in grid and cable capacity as well as so many new renewable power generators. It will need breakthroughs and expansions of battery storage, more pumped hydro, more use of hydrogen and synthetic fuels which need to be rolled out at commercial scale. There are various forecasts of costs, suggesting up to $9tn a year in the run up to 2050, with a total of more than $275 tn for transition mentioned.

Many of the areas earmarked for change will require subsidies and favourable government contracts and regulations to get started. Current products, services and fossil fuel energy have plenty of sunk investment behind them. It may well prove to be cheaper and easier to develop synthetic low or no carbon fuels to power existing machinery and vehicles than to get everyone to switch all their vehicles and equipment to new and dearer types. It is also less disruptive of people's homes and companies' factories.

So far there has been indecision about these ways to go, with more emphasis on requiring change of everything.

When it comes to the car substantial subsidy and regulatory effort has gone into getting people to buy electric cars. Little such cash and effort has gone into synthetic fuels to power existing vehicles. The decision to prefer electric cars is fraught with difficulties, as we have seen. All the time there is insufficient renewable electricity they are far from green. Meanwhile there is considerable consumer resistance.

It should be part of a green mantra that adapting what we have and extending the useful life of products that have already been made in processes emitting substantial CO 2 makes good environmental sense. Pillaging the world for the rare earths, the lithium, copper and other requirements to go to a battery driven world imposes its own strains on the planet. It also delivers economic power to China which has become dominant in many of the technologies and processes of the electrical revolution.

As much of the money to pay for all this will have to come from private sector households and companies, the improved popularity of green products is fundamental to success.

Chapter 12

Conclusions

It is becoming usual for governments to meet together to discuss how they can close down a large number of carbon-based industries in their jurisdiction. They review how they can write off the asset values of all those deposits of fossil fuels and of all those businesses that process them or rely on them to power their activities.

It is true they meet full of hope that the replacements they offer will unleash an offsetting wave of new investment and jobs. The EU itself as one of the leading architects of the green revolution is preparing programmes and subsidy budgets to tackle left behind communities that used to rely on oil wells and coal mines, on petro chemicals and on traditional industries like cement, steel and ceramics with a high use of carbon-based energy. The transition will be difficult and painful for some. There are forecasts of 200m jobs going from the fossil fuel related activities, but also estimates that new jobs in green technologies and green capital projects could exceed the losses.

As we have seen, the car and food industries are central to the changes. The existing car makers may not succeed in changing over to making enough of the new electric cars and may watch as rivals emerge with the winning products.

Agriculture will take time for many farmers to convert from animal husbandry to the new crops and to tree growing. Millions of jobs and thousands of traditional factories will be lost as investment hurries into the new fields and as the new jobs are created for those willing to train and change.

Governments would be well advised to study the successes of the digital revolution, powered by popular demand and based around friendly models of service provision and charging. Amazon took customers on a journey, gradually wooing them to the idea of paying a subscription for Amazon Prime. Google and Zoom offered free services whilst also offering enhanced services that people will pay for direct. We still await the Mini or the Beetle of the electric car revolution, the better priced domestic heating offer, and the wider range menu free of meat that attracts the many. Meanwhile governments are signing up to difficult targets for reductions in carbon dioxide. That will mean more taxes, more subsidies and more regulations controlling our lives. That will also mean more political battles as some people respond unfavourably to the demands.

There is an avalanche of investment money wanting to go into the revolution. Returns are already much reduced by the sheer weight of cash competing for the available pool of projects. Many of the large, quoted companies of the oil and gas and other traditional sectors are keen to sell on some of their fossil fuel assets and move into the new green areas, further impelling valuations of the new upwards. This will assist governments in their quest for the new paradigm.

Meanwhile the questions posed about security of supply by bad weather, military action and growing demand will need an answer. Governments need to tell us how they will fill the potential energy gap as we transition to a renewable system and need to come clean on how they will raise taxes as fossil fuels run down cutting the heavy tax revenue they carry.

Climate change itself will have its winners as well as its losers. Some places will become pleasanter as the weather warms up, whilst others will lose out from excess heat and drought. In some places more people will die of excess heat, whilst in other places fewer will die of cold in winter. The best places to farm will change as weather patterns and rainfall changes.

More attention should be given to changing the fuels used by current vehicles and industrial processes. This could prove to be a cheaper and less CO 2 intensive way of transition to a lower carbon future. Getting everyone to change the boilers, cars, factories and farms both costs far more and will generate a lot of extra CO 2 carrying through the investments. It is also high time governments themselves offered true leadership instead of adding to CO 2 by their habits of flying to conferences and running fuel inefficient offices.

Above all the joint working of governments and companies needs to reveal the range of product and changes to lifestyles that will appeal and be willingly adopted and paid for by the public. Only if a top-down revolution fires the popular imagination and becomes a bottom-up revolution will the passage to a green future be affordable and quicker. If it takes $275 tn to get there, that requires a huge number of individual and company decisions on how to spend their money in the green cause.

Printed in Great Britain
by Amazon

53577965R00050